Poetry from Past to Present

Poetry from Past to Present

BY ALBERTINE DOLORES BEACHAM

DORRANCE PUBLISHING CO., INC.
PITTSBURGH, PENNSYLVANIA 15222

The contents of this work including, but not limited to, the accuracy of events, people, and places depicted; opinions expressed; permission to use previously published materials included; and any advice given or actions advocated are solely the responsibility of the author, who assumes all liability for said work and indemnifies the publisher against any claims stemming from publication of the work.

All Rights Reserved
Copyright © 2008 by Albertine Dolores Beacham
No part of this book may be reproduced or transmitted in any form or by any means, electronic or mechanical, including photocopying, recording, or by any information storage and retrieval system without permission in writing from the publisher.

ISBN: 978-0-8059-7697-7

Printed in the United States of America

First Printing

For more information or to order additional books, please contact:
Dorrance Publishing Co., Inc.
701 Smithfield Street
Third Floor
Pittsburgh, Pennsylvania 15222
U.S.A.
1-800-788-7654
www.dorrancebookstore.com

Dedication

To Lee. Thanks for the happy years. Rest in Peace

To Whom it May Concern

I have written poetry for pleasure since I was a teen. I can remember President Nixon saying on TV., "My mother was a saint." With my mother's loving actions, I knew she was, too. So I wrote a poem about how I felt about her.

Some of the poetry I wrote was/is how my feelings were/are at the time. Some are serious, some are jovial. I've always enjoyed a good laugh and had gobs of fun writing hearty joyous humor. This is not to mock anyone—it's a figment of my imagination.

I hope you will enjoy reading my poems, as much as I've enjoyed writing them.

. . .

Because of being perceptive in my surroundings, I feel blessed with a God-given gift of seeing and having much beauty in my life.

I've put on paper, or canvas, some of it, whether it's from my family, friends, strangers, landscapes, sunsets, or music.

Who can deny the sound of a bird's lovely song, beautiful spring flowers, a snowfall, soothing rain, fall leaves, or howling winds that gently remove leaves to float them in the atmosphere.

You, too, have been given the gift to observe God's creative beauty. Enjoy it.

WHAT WOULD WE BE WITHOUT YOU?

Our military armed forces,
Your strength we always count on.
We praise you for what you strive for,
Our country that's free and strong.

You're the backbone of our country,
Our spine you keep intact.
What would we be without you?
Insecure, that's a fact.

You travel here,
You travel there.
Moving forward,
Showing you care.

Some days you face sunshine,
Others you'll face gloom.
A day you could reckon with,
The enemy soon.

Our American soldiers,
Always move straight ahead.
They stand up to the enemy,
Though cruelty they do dread.

You give us peace and comfort,
No matter what we must go through.
Standing up for our America,
And Old Glory that's red, white and blue.

Like a parent wanting to protect their child,
We ask God to stand by you.
Thank you for your honorable service,
What would we be without you?

MY MOTHER WAS A SAINT

My mother was a saint.
Her love and devotion went far.
She was a self-denying angel,
Shining brighter than a star.

She gave me birth enduring pain,
Nestled me gently in her arms.
It was not in vain, I know she'd say,
And soothe me with her charms.

My mother was a saint,
No one knew her like I did.
She sacrificed herself for me,
And for me, many tears she did shed.

When I would fumble, or couldn't tie my shoe,
She'd tell me to understand,
Many times, you'll err my child,
Now, get up, and try again.

Oh Lord, thank You for giving her to me.
Her memory will never be faint.
You gave me the best mother on earth.
My mother was a saint.

FROM MOM

Don't place me on a cloud so high,
Or think I've never gone along.
God made me a human being,
He made me weak and strong.

Show me respect, I've tried to earn,
And forgive me, when I go wrong.
I'm not a saint, can't you see?
Just mom since the day you were born.

If I were rich, or a millionaire,
And had everything money could give,
I'd offer you love and friendship
And a path on which you could live.

Sometimes I must hurt to help you.
It's only 'cause I care.
It breaks my heart when I see you stray
Off that righteous path that's there.

God gave me the privilege of having you.
I try to show my thanks each day.
One way is to do what's right for you
And mend our wrongful ways.

Don't place me so high that I will hurt you,
If you should find I've erred and sinned.
Show me love and understanding,
Should I err again.

YOU'RE THE FINEST WORK OF ART

You're the finest work of art,
That came from the heavens above.
You were made to perfection
And given to me to love.

Your stature of nobility
With morals that rang so high,
Gives you height of innocent beauty,
That goes up to the sky.

You're my masterpiece, my pride and joy,
I'm proud that you are mine.
You were made with so much tenderness,
From pebbles of love left behind.

You're the finest work of art,
That God put on earth.
I thank Him for giving you to me.
And I'm thankful for your priceless worth.

JEFFERY

Your sweetheart and you
Made plans yesterday,
To get married, the morrow,
In a church far away.

It was the place where you met,
Many years ago.
For you both to recall,
The love that did flow.

The wedding day is here.
You're dressed in your best suit,
Waiting patiently in the church,
Observing the large group.

Many hours have long passed.
Jeffery's in church all alone.
He wonders what happened,
What could have gone wrong?

With his head hanging down,
He stared at the floor,
Wondering where she was,
Did she love him anymore?

His friend saw him walking,
On the street one sunny day,
"Do you mind if I walk with you?
I'm going the same way."

As she watched him closely,
She knew how he felt,
Took his hand in hers,
Without feeling guilt.

"Jeffery, you've got a broken heart,
It's easy to see.
You've got tears in your eyes,
Where sparkles should be."

"You seem so lonely,
And you look so all alone.
I know how you feel,
Since your loved one has gone."

"You do look down,
and you seem very blue.
Jeffery, you're crying over her,
Like I cried, over you."

I'LL DREAM

Alone tonight, I'll dream of you,
Of the fun we had, when our love was new.
I'll dream tonight, of when life was gay,
Laughter filled the hours most every day.

I remember the day we said good-bye.
We both had tears, but tried not to cry.
You held me in your arms so tight,
Said, "Uncle Sam needs me to fight."

"Take care of Mom and Dad, for me,
My sister, and brother, and of course, thee.
It won't be long, before I'll be home,
Back in your arms, where I belong."

You did what you thought that you should,
Stood up to the enemy, as much as you could.
A long time passed, with no news at all.
Then two officers came, to my door to call.

I met them with my mouth agape,
Knowing, it was about your fate.
And it was, my darling, you won't be back.
God took you home, say it's not a fact.

I accept His will, but I miss you so.
Oh, my darling, I want you to know,
When you went away, you asked me to wait.
Blue skies now are grey. I know it's my fate.

When shadows fall, I'll dream of you,
Of the fun we had when our love was new.
I dream of when our life was gay,
Laughter filled the hours most every day.

You have my promise, we'll be together again.
When I meet you over there, my darling, my friend.
I wait for you, as strange as it may seem,
To be there with me, when I'll dream.

THE MAGIC NEEDLE AND THREAD

Dear angel, you have a magic needle and thread,
To mend a broken heart.
Please bring it to me as fast as you can,
I need it for another start.

I was told your needle is from Cupid's arrow,
The thread is spun from love.
The mending you do is with tender care.
You get the magic from a star above.

Bring it to me with loving care,
Let me feel its magic touch.
My heart needs mending with the needle and thread,
It needs mending very much.

Dear angel, be my guardian angel, please,
I can't go on this way.
Please bring me the magic needle and thread,
And mend my broken heart today.

THAT'S THE KIND OF PERSON YOU ARE

You give sunshine warmth, when I'm blue.
The moonbeam always follows you.
You make dull eyes, have a twinkle,
That's the kind of person you are.

A good kind of person,
A friendly kind of person,
My kind of person,
That's the kind of person you are.

You make many things right for me,
Foes you turn into harmony.
Many good things you do for free.
Thanks, from the bottom of my heart.

You bring truths, never ugly lies,
You see beauty in butterflies.
The warmth you give, I idolized.
That's the kind of person you are.

You are a nice kind of person,
A friendly kind of person.
My kind of person,
That's the kind of person you are.

SPRING HAS SPRUNG

Spring has sprung, it's in the air,
To greet us with a determined flair.
Wide awake after a winter's rest,
It strives to show us what it does best.

Spring has sprung, it's all around,
In the air, and on the ground.
For each deep breath, that we inhale,
It's fresh and soothing, never stale.

Colorful flowers and bright baby leaves,
Nesting birds, happy, in the trees.
Spring has sprung, with a special treat,
With love-bugs to bite and then retreat.

A strolling couple, under the sky so blue,
Speak endearments, not just a few.
Bride and groom, walk down the aisle,
Their parents with tears, they with a smile.

Spring has sprung,
It does each year,
With its welcoming gifts,
We treasure so dear.

THAT GOOD OLD SUMMERTIME

That good old summertime,
Takes a turn to show it's treat.
Sunshine that scintillates,
Gives warmth that can't be beat.

A time of year for school to close,
With children's happy faces.
Vacation time, full speed ahead,
The family going places.

A swim, a picnic,
Bike riding, and then,
They hop in the car,
Go see loved ones again.

Farmers drop vegetable seeds,
With hopes that they'll sprout.
That good old summertime,
Helps them pop right out.

Now that summer's long days,
Are ready to go,
Autumn paints its leaves,
For a flashy show.

When vacation time is over,
Many are bound to regret.
That good old summertime,
A time they'll never forget.

AUTUMN

She struts with pride, her resplendent beauty.
After laying down her pallet of duty.
With vanity, she invisibly steps aside,
Her talents to be viewed by those in stride.

A young couple on a winding dirt road,
Farmers with wagons, carrying their load.
Artists wanting to capture the view,
Of autumn's colors, not just a few.

Her gentle winds,
With a swish and sway,
Say I'll never leave you,
I'm here to stay.

WINTER WONDERLAND

With spring's surfing freshness,
A touch of summer's heat,
Autumn's breezy wind,
Their gifts are winter's treat.

A different kind of freshness,
From snowflakes high above.
Heat from roaring fireplaces,
With warmth for all to love.

As for the winds of autumn,
Winter uses it to show,
Its strength of cold and fierceness,
While touching the softness of the snow.

Winter gives a season of gladness,
Holidays, when guests do call.
Skiing, sledding, snowballs, and fun,
Not for one, for mostly all.

With secrets, presents, and wrappings,
Busy while welcoming the cold.
Santa visits, Winter Wonderland,
With surprises only winter holds.

TALK TO ME ABOUT LOVE

Don't talk to me about my odd shape,
Or about the tapes of Watergate.
Hold my hand for goodness sakes,
And talk to me about love.

Don't talk about my wigs, or my hair dyes,
Or about telephone bugs, that don't have eyes.
You're not here to criticize,
Just talk to me about love.

Don't go giving me sympathy,
'Cause Webster printed that word for me.
Papa! Two's just right, not three.
I'll yell if I need your help.

Honey, we were made for each other,
If I want to hold hands,
I'll get my brother. Yes, I want a fast lover.
So, talk to me about love.

Talk to me harshly,
Talk to me softly.
Talk to me anyway,
Just talk to me about love.

DON'T TALK TO ME ABOUT LOVE

Don't talk to me about walkin' and talkin',
Or about my hound-dog always barking.
You can talk about my rooster squawking,
But don't talk to me about love.

You can say to me, you're high society,
A handsome dude that's high and mighty.
Talk about the time we got high as a kite-e.
Just don't talk to me about love.

You can hold my hand, sit on my lap.
Pet my dog, now scratch my back.
Pucker your lips, you're on the right track.
Keep it up, baby, we're getting things right.

You can talk and really go too far,
Just don't harass me, leave things as they are.
I never wanted things perfect, by gar,
So don't talk to me about love.

WATCH IT BABY

Watch it, baby, your spark is getting cold again.
Our amber glow is dying, like it's playing in the rain.
If you want things right, you better heat up tonight.
So watch it, baby, your spark is getting cold again.

You'd always bring me sunshine,
Whenever you'd appear.
The sun turned into snowflakes,
With a chill in the air.

You think I cannot feel it,
Or see it on your face,
That fire we had a burning,
Has gone another place.

I'm gonna start a looking,
To find me a flame.
So watch it, baby,
Your spark is getting cold again.

I'M GONNA GET DOLLED UP

You just wait and see, honey,
Your baby went and got mad.
Now, I'm gonna get dolled up,
And have the best time I've ever had.

I'll shop for new clothes today,
And a blond wig that's long and just right.
I'll change my glass eye tomorrow,
It'll flutter when a man's in sight.

I've got some new false teeth ordered,
They're gonna be the brightest sight.
I'm having them custom made, you know,
So they will glow all through the night.

I won't need pills to get high on,
Or booze to get me lit,
'Cause when I get my new duds,
I'll be all that, and some yet.

My hair will blow with the breeze,
My raven blue eyes will flutter.
When I show my glowing smile,
I'll have you men melting like butter.

So you just wait and see, honey,
You'll be sorry you walked out like that.
When you see that I'm all dolled up,
I know you'll come running right back.

MY HEART'S DESIRE

I walked out on you, darling,
I wanted fun and living strong.
I was searching to find happiness,
I wanted to make it alone.

I've been moving around from town to town,
Looking for my heart's desire.
I had lots of class with my fancy friends,
I was so hot, I was burning like fire.

Some nights I'd go out dancing,
Other times I'd sit and cry.
`Cause no matter how hard I really tried,
I couldn't find my heart's desire.

I did a lot of hot loving,
While I was stepping out at night.
But my thoughts kept slipping back to you,
Of the times I held you tight.

When I walked out on you, darling,
Forgive me, I was so wrong.
I found the happiness I was looking for,
I found I left it at home.

LET'S SMOKE A PEACE PIPE

Let's smoke a peace pipe, my darling,
I'm ready to make peace with you.
I'll be your match,
And light us up,
Let's smoke, I'm feeling blue.

I've cried a lot, and walked the floor.
Let's forgive once more.
Let's smoke a peace pipe, my darling,
I'm ready to make peace with you.

Let's smoke and blow away our anger and schemes,
And blow 'til it turns into loving smoke rings.
We can place them on our fingers that are bare,
And get back together to show that we care.

My darling, please, will you forgive me?
The love I have, is for only thee.
Lets smoke a peace pipe, my darling,
I'm ready to make peace with you.`

I'M A POLLY TICKIN' MAMA

We can smoke a peace pipe, my darling,
'Cause you agreed to let me stand,
And do the things I want to do,
For the good old USA land.

You see, I've watched those politics,
Some sure need straightened out.
I'm gonna do the best I can,
And show that I've got clout.

Here's the way it really is,
Politics run the land.
They think that they can do no wrong,
We sure need a honest hand.

I live in a place called USA,
It's part of a politicking world.
I love it much, but at times it gets strange,
'Specially when some things reach a boil.

They've got some of the best strategies,
The best I ever saw.
Granny says they use psychology,
She says that's stuff from an old slop jar.

Look at the first president of out country,
His politicking will make you whirl,
Right now it's the year 2007,
And we've never had a president girl.

I'm a politicking mama,
All the way from Californ'.
I just love knowing politics,
'Cause they really turn me on.

Some of his footsteps were called:
Lyndon, Dick, Clinton, and Bush is taking a whirl.
When I look at all the politicking they did,
I'm damn glad I was born a girl.

Lyndon went straight to heaven,
His strategy got him resting in peace.
While he was alive he smiled a lot at the girls,
Ooh, I loved that politicking tease.

Dicky, you were such a naughty boy,
For making those tapes squeal.
You should've studied more politicking,
And crossed them up on their reel.

And you, Clinton, you did your best,
To hide a secret you held dear.
But the damn thing slipped right through the cracks,
So, on the couch you went for a year.

Bush, baby, you really did your best,
Many said you did things wrong.
Like all presidents, you thought you tried,
To make our country strong.

You have all turned me on,
For ticking in your own way.
But don't step down to a girl,
If you want politicking to stay.

To the new leader of the USA,
Be a good example for your brothers,
A hell of a lot depends on you,
Don't get caught like all the others!

I'm a politicking mama,
I'm on my way to Washington.
I'm gonna help you all do your stuff,
For a little politicking fee!

OUR UNITED STATES OF AMERICA

Our United States of America,
Home of those that strive for liberty.
Her strength and courage moves on and on,
It comes; from you and me.

I'll never look down on my country,
For an error one might have done,
Instead, I work harder with all of you,
Our mistakes to be overcome.

As I see Old Glory waving,
I feel strength, courage, and pride.
It makes me feel so secure,
With a loving feeling inside.

I ask God to let her always wave,
Over our country, so brave and free.
Let other countries to take steps,
To be free, like you and me.

I place trust in the leadership of our country,
They all try hard to keep our country great.
Oh, thank you, Lord, for the gift you gave.
Our America, our United States!

THAT'S THE REASON I WANT YOU

I'm just a poor girl, with a rich girl's taste.
That's the reason I want you.
I want the best on earth, to quench my rich thirst,
Not any drink of water will do.

All the money or material things won't do.
For me to be rich, I've gotta have you.
I'm just a poor girl, with a rich girl's taste.
That's the reason I want you.

I don't want diamonds or furs or fancy new cars,
'Cause I'll be rich having you, just like you are.
I'm just a poor girl, with a rich girl's taste.
That's the reason I want you.

PASS THE JUG AROUND

Friend, I'm on the water wagon,
After my spree and wild whoopee.
You see, I painted the whole town red,
And made all kinds of history.

We were downing booze from my friend's jug,
I planned to make that girl quiet fast.
When my Russian hands started to roam,
My gal knocked me flat on my yass.

I said, come here, my little baby,
Let us get a little more booze.
It makes us kinda forget ourselves,
And do things not allowed in school.

Ooh, my woozy head is aching bad,
My drinking and gal sure did clash,
I'm also hurting in other spots,
'Cause my gal knocked me flat on my yass.

Yes, friend, pass the jug around,
Get a swig and get it quick.
Pass the jug around, pass the jug around,
But not to me, no more, I quit!

ARE YOU CRYING OVER OUR BREAKUP?

While you're looking out your window,
Tears are falling from your eyes.
Are you crying over our breakup,
Hoping our love never dies?

Do you see me as you are looking,
At the twinkling stars above?
Do you wish that you could hold me,
As one holds the one he loves?

Are you trying to tell me something,
Maybe that you do care?
Are you crying over our breakup,
And our old love affair?

Would you mind if I came to you,
To help pave the way?
Could I meet you accidentally,
On the street across the way?

Will you kiss my eyes gently,
And tell me that you care?
If you're crying over our breakup,
Then meet me, darling, I'll be there.

IF YOU SAY FROG, BABY

If you say frog, baby,
I'll leap mighty high for you.
Call me your worm, honey,
And I'll wiggle when you want me to.

I'll be your fish,
And swim the ocean blue.
I'll flop from the pan,
To the fire for you.

You can call me your kitten,
You can call me your dove.
I'll purr when you stroke me,
And coo when we make love.

We can play monkey see,
We can play monkey do.
Any game you want to play,
I'll play along with you.

If you say frog, baby,
I'll leap down the aisle for you,
Make me your wife, baby,
And I'll surprise you with a thing or two.

THE HONEYMOON'S OVER

The honeymoon's over, baby,
Things are gonna change a lot.
I bowed down to you before,
Whether I liked it or not.

Now that we are married,
We need to get a few things straight.
A spouse has privileges,
And for those, I refuse to wait.

Yesterday you shouted frog at me,
Expecting me to leap mighty high.
I didn't, then you called me a worm,
So I wiggled and blackened your eye.

Now listen to me, baby,
I'm sure we're gonna get along.
You see, my pa was a wrestler,
And he was mighty strong.

He saw how you treated me,
and said I was a fool,
So he taught me how to defend myself,
With ways he didn't learn in school.

I've been doing a lot of reading,
Things have changed over the years.
A spouse no longer has a master,
So, the honeymoon's over, dear.

Be gentle when we're together,
Don't order me around,
'Cause that could be disastrous,
With you sprawled out on the ground.

The honeymoon is over, baby,
That's something you shouldn't forget.
I'll strive to make our marriage work,
Meet me half-way, or live in regret.

I LOVE YOU MOST

I love morning dewdrops, swaying trees,
Seashores, seashells, bumble bees,
A soft kitten, and your company.
But did you know, I love you most?

I love the way you walk.
I love the way you talk.
I want to go the places you go
And do the things you do.

I love high peak mountains
And sloping hills,
The postman to pass and leave no bills.
But did you know, I love you most?

I've met many handsome men,
Your party friends, and their host.
When I compare them to you,
Darling, I love you most.

THAT'S THE TRUTH, AND I'M STICKING TO IT

Pa's late coming home after drinking,
I'll tell you it just ain't fair.
The whoppers he always tells my Ma,
Each one has a different flair.

Does she really believe him?
I guess, 'cause she writes it down,
She has a whole book of his excuses,
From when he was out on the town.

I've heard a lot of different tales,
Coming from his smooth talking ways.
But I think things are gonna change,
If she wakes up from her daze.

Ma is like an angel,
She listens to his talk, so thick,
Before her lecture, he thinks,
"I need a story, and need it quick."

"I was gonna come home early,
But the building caught on fire.
Had a hellova time putting it out,
It caused customers a lot of dire."

"Well, if that's the case, my husband,
It's perfume I smell, not smoke.
Start talking and explain that one.
Get the words out, no need to poke."

"Well, it's like this, my dear,
I stopped off for a bit of booze.
When the smoke and flames surrounded me,
My life I thought I'd lose."

"Don't give me all that bull,
You know that's just not so.
There's no smoke odor, just perfume.
Your tales just seem to grow."

"The firemen started working,
What happened was so awful.
They soon ran out of water,
And what they did wasn't lawful."

"Next door was a perfume factory,
My bright idea was a hit.
They used perfume and put the fire out
That's the truth, and I'm sticking to it!"

"Now darling I'm telling you the truth this time,
I'm not drunk, just a little lit.
You can believe me if you want to,
I need my bed, I feel mighty sick."

"How come you don't smell like smoke,
Only perfume and your booze?"
"Wife, that perfume overpowers smoke,
Believe me, if you choose."

Pa went to bed that night,
The next week he was out again.
He came home looking a wreck,
Ma's kisses gave him a spin.

The next day with all her dough,
She said, "I put your tales in my book.
You caused me to win the lying contest,
That's the truth, and I'm sticking to it!"

OLD AND FEEBLE

Pa is old and feeble.
Ma takes good care of him.
Sometimes he slips out to roam,
Finding him is usually slim.

Upset, she calls the police,
Trembling, she says her man is gone.
He slipped out while she was sleeping,
Unyielding, as he roams alone.

Now Pa and Ma aren't wealthy,
They barely make ends meet.
Their credit standing is great,
Used only for a special need.

With him being feeble,
He bought without a second thought,
A new car and new furniture,
And that was only the very start.

He went home just a smiling,
"Look at what I just bought.
I put it all on our credit card,
I did very good, I thought."

"Oh my God, what have you done,
When you slipped out this time?
There's no money to pay for that,
Not paying bills is a crime."

She planned to try to take them back,
 He thought he did really good.
But being old and feeble,
He doesn't do just what he should.

While she slept he found her purse,
And removed all the cash.
Trying to get to the store for tickets,
Before they closed, he made a dash.

He spent it on tickets for the lottery,
Happily he returned back home.
He placed the tickets on her pillow,
As a surprise he got while he roamed.

His wife found the tickets,
Upset. "What have you done?
We can't afford those tickets,
Every bit of our money is gone!"

She tried to be calm about it,
Knowing he was old and feeble.
She did love him, no matter what,
She'll care for him, long as she's able.

She threw the tickets on the kitchen table,
Planning to throw them away.
She decided to watch the drawings,
Shock hit her in every way.

One ticket was a winner,
For more money she'd never known.
She paid for the things he bought before,
Determined, no more he'll bring home.

She hired a man her husband liked,
To stay by him each day.
To stop him from buying things,
And to keep him from going astray.

She thinks of all their riches,
Now she can finally pay off the bills.
He doesn't realize he won the lottery,
'Cause he's old and feeble, he never will.

Each other, is what they had,
Through thickness and through thin.
Love is keeping them together,
Until the very end.

OUR LOVE FOR EACH OTHER

A devoted man had a family,
Children, and a wife at home.
He spent his days at work,
Until his duties were done.

After work he drove to his house,
A proud husband and dad was he.
When they all rushed to greet him,
Made him as happy as can be.

One day it was sunny and great,
He rushed home from work to be
With them, to go on an outing
In their boat, to sail on the sea.

When he got a block away,
He started shaking as he cried.
"Smoke is coming from our house,"
He couldn't wait to get inside.

He screamed to his family,
"You're my life, I've got to find you!
Frantic, he crawled and found them,
And knew just what to do.

He stretched them out on the lawn,
Fell to the ground, by their side,
A fire-truck and neighbors went to them.
To see if they were alive.

On their way to the hospital,
They fought to save their life,
Went straight to emergency,
He, his children, and wife.

After a few days of treatment,
They were all doing great.
But they had no house to go to,
The fire had taken it away.

While tears were being shed,
Over the treasures that they had.
The husband, told his family,
"You're my treasure, don't feel bad."

"We have so much to be thankful for.
Our lives have been spared.
The house is just a material thing,
Another, I know can be had."

"I know it won't be the same,
It held treasures we loved dear.
Photos and things can't be replaced,
But, look at us, we're still here!"

The family circled the husband,
Cuddled him in their arms,
"Our love for each other,
Will get us through many storms."

THE BUM

There was an old bum who was homeless,
No folks he had, he did dread.
He strolled by day to find shelter,
Any place to rest his head.

His life wasn't easy,
He learned ways to live,
On things from the forest,
Or what kind folks would give.

He knew what greens were edible,
Some meat he ate, you'd frown.
'Cause some came from high above,
And some crawling on the ground.

He'd rob a bird's nest when he could,
For their eggs he loved to eat.
Unfortunately, they were so little,
It was only a small treat.

Observing a rattlesnake a crawling,
Close by his worn out shoes,
He had his stick awaiting,
While he pretended to snooze.

Suddenly, he lifted the stick,
Hit the snake in the right spot,
Then he smiled from ear to ear,
For the delicious meal he got.

A week passed, and he had no meat.
He was laying on the ground.
When suddenly he saw a buzzard flying
Over him, going round and round.

He took a long look at the bird,
Flying close to him when it could.
I guess not being able to bathe,
The buzzard thought he was food.

The bum was startled by the buzzard,
The first time one came about.
It made him angry, it wanted him to eat,
"I'll reverse that, without a doubt."

He got his sling-shot ready,
With a rock as sharp as a tack,
He said, "I think I'll have fun,
That bird doesn't know the fact."

Buzzard, buzzard, in the air,
How come you're flying over there?
Before I had rattlesnake,
Today I'm gonna have Buzzard steak."

He aimed at the buzzard.
It fell close to his feet.
"I never had buzzard steak before,
But to me, meat is meat."

He cleaned it in the lake,
Got it roasted, and it smelled good.
While he was eating it, he said, "Buzzard,
How does it feel to be eaten for food?"

It was the first time the bum ate buzzard.
He was proud of how it cooked.
It made a mighty tasty meal,
A hellova lot better than it looked.

LIKE IT USED TO BE

The house was sitting in the middle of town,
A more beautiful one couldn't be found.
Flowers in the yard of every hue,
Sporting their beauty for all to view.

It wore a coat of cream so bright,
Pale green trim, set it off just right.
Constant beauty, with their flairs,
The porch held two rocking chairs.

A man in one, his wife in the other,
Rocked, as they chatted about the weather.
Their dog by his feet, the cat in her lap,
While they talked, the animals took a nap.

As time passed, their actions grew slow,
Glen's hair was gray, Mary's white as snow.
They slowly lost strength, as they aged,
The neglected house, saw better days.

Glen took to his bed, and soon he was gone,
She had everything to do, she was alone.
Their beautiful house, that used to be,
Is a rambling shack, for all to see.

Mary decided, to not sit home and mope,
She wanted friends and needed hope.
She took her time and dressed up good,
Made her way to church the best she could.

Leaning on her cane, limping on the way,
To the church they went to, many a day.
Tears flooded her eyes, as she was greeted,
Embraced by friends, that she really needed.

Soon they were chatting, about back when
They were young and strong, then they'd grin.
She made cookies and cakes for many in town,
And helped those she could, before she got down.

Soon friends went to call, they remembered those days,
When she showed her kindness, in so many ways.
The children now grown, and those strong and alert,
Went to Mary they loved, her house to convert.

Back to the prettiest house in town,
It wore the same colors all around.
The framework repaired, a brand new door,
They worked in the yard, made it like before,

Mary pleased, over what her friends did
With a great big grin, her tears weren't hid.
She walked around, hoping Glen could see,
Friends made the house, like it used to be.

LIFE MUST GO ON

Sitting alone in her old rocking chair,
The one beside, her, is now bare.
She reminisced about the man she wed,
Who went to Heaven, leaving his deathbed.

A big smile crossed her old wrinkled face,
Thinking about his loving embrace.
Remembering happiness they shared,
A gentle touch, to show that they cared.

She knows that life can sometimes be cruel,
We've all got to die, that's not a self-rule.
When the time comes, we're sad and shaken,
To realize our loved one, has been taken.

An old song that he sang, made lots of sense,
It was about when some crossed the fence.
Of how family and those left behind,
Could help them to sooth their grieving minds.

"Remember the good days, forget the bad,
Think of the happiness, that you shared.
You'll cry and grieve, then go on soon,
'Cause life must go as usual."

HIS SNORE

How I wish that I could hear once more,
My husband's old familiar snore.
His snore that kept me awake at night,
When everything else was very quiet.
I'm all alone, snuggled in my bed,
The quietness, I really do dread.
'Cause all I do is concentrate,
On the nights his snores kept me awake.
I have always thought them a great bore,
Now, I wish that I could hear them more.

GREG

Greg lives in the country, all alone.
In a large, sprawling house, he calls home.
While on the porch, he thinks of the past,
The happiness they shared, the many laughs.

His wife was Bertha, understanding and kind.
Passed, and left her family behind.
Four daughters to raise, and a handsome son,
A handful for a man, with a household to run.

He did what he could, was green from the start.
Little by little, wisdom he caught.
There were rules to follow, he tried to be fair,
Yet, many times he'd shout, "Don't you dare!"

Years passed, and he did what he could,
To raise his children to be kind and good.
They made errs, like all families make,
But their love for each other, was no mistake.

They grew up fast, went out a with a friend,
Greg watched closely, as romances began.
They flew the coup, as marriage took place,
Soon they gave an increase, to the human race.

It's Christmas time, and Greg's alone,
He observes his quiet living room.
"This room needs to look lived in,
I'll get my gear, and then begin.

He put on his coat, got his axe,
Said, "This is no time, for me to relax."
He hobbled in the woods, like before.
To find a tree, his family would adore.

When the tree was in, he wanted to flee,
He didn't know how, to decorate the tree.
To get it beautiful, was mighty slim,
'Cause Bertha and the kids did all the trim.

He put on the lights and then stood back,
"I'm doing it by golly, I'm on the right track."
With a box full of bulbs, he hung on the tree,
With tears, he whispered, "It's for only me."

He stood back and admired, the beauty it had,
But being alone to enjoy it, made him sad.
They have families and celebrate at home,
Just like we did, before they were gone.

He put on Christmas music and sat in a chair,
Listening and understanding, with a silent prayer.
I know they're happy, I did what I could,
They're out on their own, like families should.

Greg listened to the music, loud and clear,
Remembering the time when they all were there.
Wishing he could turn time back to when,
He could have his family home, once again.

He didn't know, coming down the road,
Was a caravan of cars, carrying a load.
His dog, Chip, left his side,
Ran to the door, barking as he cried.

Greg got up to see what was wrong,
Said, "Chip, they're home where they belong."
But Chip scratched on the door, to go out,
Then Greg saw the cars, without a doubt.

With teary eyes, and thinking, so glad,
"I'm gonna have the best Christmas I ever had."
Out on the road, he ran to them.
Their hugs and kisses were poured on him.

Once inside, they put gifts under the tree,
Greg said, "Dear Lord, I do thank Thee."
Laughing and talking near the tree,
Just like he wished and hoped it would be.

Christmas is over, they're long gone,
To their own homes, where they belong.
"I'll cherish forever, the gift they left behind,
Memories of my family, that turned out mighty fine."

A FACTUAL SOLDIER'S TRANSFER

Just before Christmas, a soldier got orders,
To relocate to another post, and get new quarters.
With a spouse and five children, ready to leave,
The last day of school, was more important they believed.

In school, after the party, the class was ready to go,
A child started crying, "We don't have a tree to show."
Sympathy touched, the teacher and the class,
They decided the tree, would go to the crying lass.

She skipped from the room, to the car that was packed,
Smiling happily, carrying the tree on her back.
Her father took one look, at the tree and said,
"What I must tell you, I really do dread."

"There's no room in our car, we're carrying a load,
Take that tree right back, we've gotta hit the road."
The children started crying, "We won't have a tree,
For Santa to put toys under, we all agree."

They quickly got sympathy, and Pa did agree,
To try to find room, for the Christmas tree.
In the station wagon, he removed the duffel bags,
Tied them on top, with what little rope he had.

They got in the wagon, and soon were on their way,
To the new post, almost a week away.
Happily they sang carols, to keep the kids calm,
They heard a thump, and the duffel bags were gone.

The highway was crowded, with cars speeding by,
No time to worry, no time to cry.
The wagon backed up, and pulled over to the side,
Father got the duffel bags, to prevent a collide.

With the bags in the wagon, the tree over them,
The chance of them falling, was mighty slim.
Once again they started, out on their way,
Arrived at the motel, to spend Christmas day.

The tree with decorations, and a bright shiny star,
Pleased the traveling family, that they brought it in the car.
They were tucked into bed, soon sleeping sound,
Knowing Santa Claus would soon be around.

The tree lights blinked throughout night,
Santa left presents, then slipped out of sight.
The children aroused, happy as can be,
To see what they got, under the Christmas tree.

They spent Christmas day in the motel room,
Laughing and playing, no time for gloom.
The next day they were happily on their way,
To their new home, where, for a while they'll stay.

SANTA'S SLEIGH IS ON THE WAY

Yeah, hey, hey, Santa's on his way.
He's got with him, a big bag of toys.
Oh, ho, ho, just gotta let you know,
His goodies, are for good girls and boys.

Santa's sleigh is on the way, I know, I know.
Santa and his friends are coming soon.
Hear him laughing, oh, ho, ho, ho, ho, ho.
Santa's sleigh is on the way I know.

Hear the bells, that's Santa's little elves.
Ringing cheer with Mister Jolly Clown.
Hear the horn, that's Scarecrow in the corn,
He's blowing this Christmas tune for you.

Yeah, hey, hey, Santa's on his way,
He's got with him a big bag of toys.
Oh, ho, ho, just gotta let you know,
His goodies are for good girls and boys.

You're snuggled in bed, good thoughts in your head.
With visions of Santa's big show.
He's coming to you, with goodies tonight.
Santa's sleigh is on the way, I know.

MERRY CHRISTMAS EVERYBODY

Merry Christmas everybody. Merry Christmas.
Smile and be on your merry way.
Christmas comes but once a year,
Celebrate your best today.

Many years ago in a manger,
Lay and an infant great, but small.
His birth started our Christmases,
With gifts brought to the stall.

A shining star led the way,
For viewers to appear.
When baby Jesus was born to Holy Mary,
The most sacred day of any year.

Merry Christmas, everybody. Merry Christmas.
Let's celebrate that great day
With food and toys and gifts for joy,
Be merry, and give thanks in your way.

Merry Christmas, everybody. Merry Christmas.
It's so nice to see you smile today.
Pebbles of yuletide cheer surrounding us,
Aglow for our Savior's Day.

Merry Christmas, everybody. Merry Christmas.

CHRISTMAS IS COMING, OUR FATHER

Christmas is coming, our Father,
Please won't you hear my prayer?
Let us have a Merry Christmas,
Grant our loved ones all be there.

Our Father who art in Heaven,
Please listen to my plea.
We bear a heavy burden,
It's one many do not see.

Let us have a Merry Christmas.
Give everyone the privilege to be free.
Let us change our mistakes to righteousness,
And I thank You for understanding me.

Christmas is coming, our Father,
Let my loved ones be home once more.
Let me hear their happy laughter,
And their footsteps on the floor.

Oh Lord, you did not make us perfect,
We on this earth do sin.
Grant us wisdom to understand ourselves,
And the mistakes we'll make again.

Christmas is coming, our Father,
Bless our home and all on earth,
Please let us profit by our mistakes,
And place love above material worth.

Dear Lord, please let us profit by our mistakes,
And place love above material worth.